Ready-to-Go
Phonics

by Cheryl Potts

SCHOLASTIC
PROFESSIONAL BOOKS

New York ❧ Toronto ❧ London ❧ Auckland ❧ Sydney
New Delhi ❧ Mexico City ❧ Hong Kong

A special thanks to Fran Sortman for inspiring and challenging me to create phonics materials for her classroom.

Thanks also to Tania Moore, Diane Watkins, Patricia Clark, Vicki Harrington, Sherrie Everett, and Jackie Peabody for inviting me to their classrooms to share phonics fun and games with their students.

And thanks to Judy Grant, Julé Lattimer and Roxanne Ferguson for their encouragement and support as fellow writers.

※

Edited by Wiley Blevins
Cover design by Pamela Simmons and Jaime Lucero
Cover photos by Bob Lorenz
Cover and interior illustrations by Maxie Chambliss
Interior design by Pamela Simmons

※

ISBN 0-590-11594-4

gl fr a th st e tr pl i ch sk o gr ol u wh sp

Contents

About This Book 4

Alphabet Recognition

Alphabet Ringtoss 7

Alphabet Tic-tac-toe 8

I'm Thinking of… 9

Alphabet Magic Hat 10

Line 'Em Up 12

Consonants, Clusters, and Digraphs

Consonant Quizzer 13

Soft *c* & *g* Rhyme Bookmarks 15

Consonant Corner 16

Concentration 17

Blend Match-a-Roo 19

Blend-O 23

Digraph Rhyme 25

Digraph Puzzlers 26

Vowels

Vowel Cheers 29

Short & Long Vowels 32

Vowel Picture Cards 37

Vowel Spellings 38

Pick 'n' Peek 39

Contents

(continued)

Old MacDonald's Vowel Farm 45

Vowel Clip It 46

Vowel-in-the-Middle 50

Treasure Sock 53

Say It and Slot It 54

Silent-*e* Game 56

Word Score 60

Diphthong Song 62

Dial-a-Diphthong 63

Mr. Drew 67

The Yarn Game 68

Word Analysis

The ABC's of Compound Words 72

Compound Art 73

Compound Comedy 74

Contraction Pop-Ups 76

Contraction Toss 77

Syllable Search 78

Classroom Resources

Classroom Resources 80

About This Book

Welcome to *Ready-to-Go Phonics*. I wrote this book after years of searching for fun, meaningful ways to teach my students valuable reading skills. Activities, games, manipulatives, and rhymes have not only provided my students with hours of "playful learning" but have given them important tools to figure out unknown words. Readers use several strategies to figure out unknown words. These strategies include:

- **phonics**
- **picture clues**
- **context clues**
- **sight words**

Phonics involves the relationship between sounds and their spellings. The ability to connect sounds to spellings is one of the most important strategies early readers use to decode words. The engaging poems, easy-to-make games, and purposeful learning center activities in *Ready-to-Go Phonics* are designed to help you strengthen your students' ability to use phonics skills to make sense of the printed word—and to make learning fun! These activities can be used to teach, review, and reinforce phonics skills in whole-class or small-group settings and can be integrated into your regular reading and spelling programs.

Periodically review with your students all the decoding strategies. When they encounter unknown words while reading, assist students in fully analyzing the words and thinking about the many ways to decode them. Model for your students the most appropriate strategy or strategies in the given situation. The flexible use of all these strategies will help in developing strong, fluent readers.

What's Inside

Each activity and game in this book takes you from preparation to extensions. Here's an overview of what each lesson includes:

- **Skill** the phonics focus in the particular game or activity

- **Players** the recommended number of players in each game group or activity

- **Materials** a complete list of all materials needed; each game includes reproducible pages with game boards and cards, plus spinners and number cubes as necessary

- **Getting Ready** complete preparation how-to's with helpful management tips to make activities go smoothly

- **How to Play** step-by-step directions to share with students

- **Phonics Fact** a definition of the phonics term being focused on in the lesson

- **Variations** suggestions for making the game or activity easier or more challenging or for adapting it to other phonics skills

- **Teacher Corner** extension activities to reinforce particular phonics skills

- **Literature Links** suggested books and poems that demonstrate the phonics skill being focused on in the lesson

Helpful Hints

The following suggestions will help you adapt the games and activities for your class:

❧ Enlarge game boards, cards, and other game pieces on a photocopier. For added durability, paste game boards onto larger pieces of colored construction paper before coloring and laminating. Paste word and picture cards onto index cards and laminate.

❧ Designate an area in your classroom for phonics. I suggest setting up a bulletin board filled with phonics generalizations, word lists, and activities. Below the bulletin board, place a table. Stock it with games, center activities, and books for practicing phonics skills in context. Establish a routine so that students have opportunities to visit the phonics area at least twice a week for independent or small-group work.

❧ Select activities from this book that fit your teaching style and your students' learning styles. For example, word lists are ideal for visual learners (see Diphthong Song, page 62), raps and rhymes help auditory learners (see Old MacDonald's Vowel Farm, page 45), and games suit kinesthetic learners (see Digraph Puzzlers, page 26).

❧ Also select the activities that best address your students' needs. The activities in the book get progressively more complex—beginning with alphabet recognition activities and progressing to a study of consonants, consonant clusters, consonant digraphs, short vowels, long vowels, variant vowels, diphthongs, and finally to word analysis skills such as compound words, contractions, and syllabication. However, most of the activities can be adapted to review phonics skills other than those designated. Suggestions are included throughout.

❧ Most of all, create an environment in which your students are actively analyzing and thinking about words. Phonics instruction should be playful and engaging. Students will enjoy the activities in *Ready-to-Go Phonics* so much they won't even realize how much they're learning!

Home-School Connection

You might find it helpful to make extra games so that children can take them home to play with family members. Getting families involved in their children's growing literacy development will have tremendous payoffs. With each game you send home, attach a note explaining the game's purpose, providing directions for its play, and offering suggestions for additional related learning opportunites. Large self-closing plastic bags make handy carrying cases.

Alphabet Ringtoss

Skill: alphabet recognition
Players: 2

Materials

large box lid
white construction paper
scissors
paste
black marker
10 small plastic bracelets, such as those found in party
    supply or novelty stores (or use pipe cleaners
    twisted into rings or "O" rings)

Getting Ready

🌀 Cut and paste the white construction paper to fit the inside of the box lid. If desired, decorate the outside of the box lid with colorful self-adhesive paper.

🌀 Write upper- and lowercase letters on the white construction paper using a thick black marker.

🌀 Place the completed box lid on the floor.

How to Play

1 Each player selects five plastic arm bracelets (rings).

2 Players take turns throwing one bracelet into the box lid and naming each letter the bracelet touches or surounds. One point is scored for each correct answer. The game continues until each player tosses all five bracelets. The player with the most points at the end of the game wins.

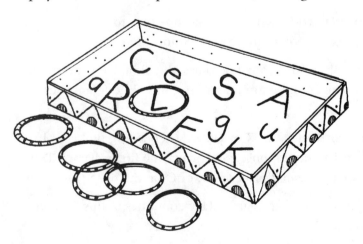

Teacher Corner

For primary-age students, it's helpful to provide daily alphabet recognition exercises. The following quick and engaging activities can be used to develop alphabet recognition:

Letter Hold-Up
Have children sit in a circle. Distribute one alphabet card to each child. As you sing "The Alphabet Song," ask each child to hold up his or her card as the letter's name is sung.

Name Card Call-Out
During the first few days of school, use children's name tags as a means of lining up for lunch, recess, or a special class such as music. Hold up an alphabet card and ask those children whose names begin with that letter to line up. Continue until all children have lined up.

ABC Books
Read a new ABC book to children every week. Allow children an opportunity to look at the pictures and identify objects whose names contain a specific sound. Place these books in your reading corner or classroom library.

Alphabet Tic-tac-toe

Skill: alphabet recognition
Players: whole class or small groups

Materials

tagboard
black marker
large brass fasteners
masking tape
36 small unlined index cards
hole punch

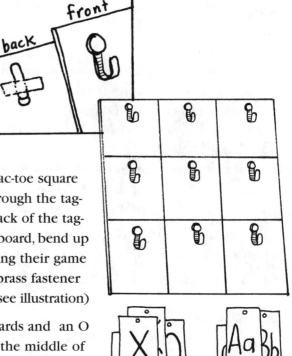

Getting Ready

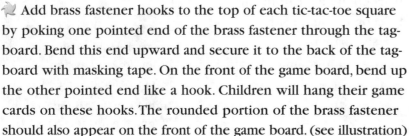 On a large piece of tagboard, use a
marker to draw the lines of a tic-tac-toe board.

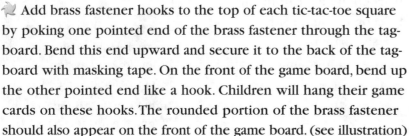 Add brass fastener hooks to the top of each tic-tac-toe square
by poking one pointed end of the brass fastener through the tag-
board. Bend this end upward and secure it to the back of the tagboard with masking tape. On the front of the game board, bend up
the other pointed end like a hook. Children will hang their game
cards on these hooks. The rounded portion of the brass fastener
should also appear on the front of the game board. (see illustration)

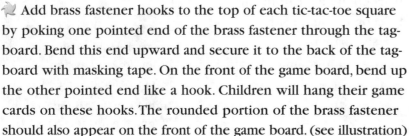 Using a black marker, draw an X on five index cards and an O
on another set of five cards. Then punch a hole in the middle of
each card near the top.

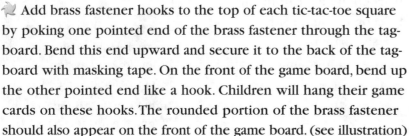 Make a set of alphabet cards using the remaining 26 index
cards. One uppercase and one lowercase letter should appear on
each card.

How to Play

1 Divide the class into two groups, or play with two smaller groups of 4 to 5 children.
Hand out the X or O cards to each team so that one team is X and the other is O.

2 Display an alphabet card to the first player on Team 1, and ask the child to name the letter
on the card or the sound the letter stands for. Team members can help one another, but
the first player must say the letter or sound.

3 If the player responds correctly, he or she places an X or O card (depending on his or her
team) anywhere on the tic-tac-toe board. If the response is incorrect, the first player on Team 2
gets that turn. If his or her response is correct, Team 2 places an X or O on the tic-tac-toe board.

4 Then repeat steps 2 and 3 with the next player on Team 2. Play continues in this fashion
until a team gets tic-tac-toe, three-in-a-row!

8

gl fr a th st e tr pl i ch sk o gr cl u wh sp

I'm Thinking of...

Skill: alphabet recognition/sound-letter correspondence
Players: whole class

Materials
small unlined index cards

Getting Ready
🐦 Write one consonant on each index card. Make one card for each child in your class. If necessary, make extra cards for the consonants most frequently found in words—*s, t, m, f, r, b, l.*

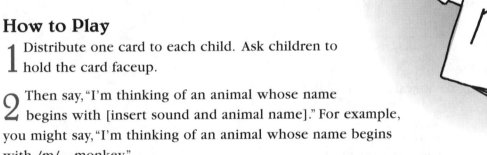

How to Play

1 Distribute one card to each child. Ask children to hold the card faceup.

2 Then say, "I'm thinking of an animal whose name begins with [insert sound and animal name]." For example, you might say, "I'm thinking of an animal whose name begins with /m/—monkey."

3 The child who has the "m" letter card displays the card, names the letter, and repeats the sound the letter stands for. Play continues until all children have displayed their cards.

Alphabet Magic Hat

Skill: alphabet recognition/sound-letter correspondence
Players: whole class

Materials

cardboard oatmeal box
black construction paperl
large paper plate
scissors
tape
16 small unlined index cards
animal game cards (see page 11)
thin black marker
glue

Variation

❋ Use old workbook pictures or stickers to make a set of cards showing other animals, toys, or classroom objects.

a gl e fr i th o st u

Getting Ready

❧ Cover the cardboard oatmeal box with black construction paper.

❧ Use the paper plate to trace and cut out a circle from black construction paper. Center the oatmeal box on this circle, then trace around it and cut out the center circle. Slip this "hat brim" over the open end of the box. Tape it in place.

❧ Copy and cut out the animal game cards, then paste them to the index cards—one per card. With a thin black marker, write the animal's name on the back of the card. Place the cards in the hat.

How To Play

1 Have children watch as you "pull an animal out of the hat." Then say, "Look what animal I pulled out of the hat . . . /g/—goat."

2 Ask children to raise their hands if they know what letter the animal name (goat) begins with. Call on a volunteer to name that letter.

3 If the child is unsure, point to and state the first letter of the animal's name on the back of the card. Continue until each child has had a turn.

Alphabet Magic Hat
Game Cards

fr a th st e tr pl i ch sk o gr cl u wh sp

Line 'Em Up

Skill: ABC order
Players: 4 to 6

Materials

52 milk jug lids (or tagboard circles)
black marker
two manila envelopes
masking tape

Geting Ready

🐾 Using a black marker, label 26 milk jug lids with upper-case letters from *A* to *Z*. Once the ink has dried, place the lids in a manila envelope for storage.

🐾 Label the remaining 26 lids with lowercase letters from *a* to *z* and place them in a separate manila envelope.

How to Play

1 Place a long strip of masking tape on the floor in front of each group of 2 to 3 children.

2 Randomly place one set of lids (uppercase or lower-case) above the masking tape strip for each group. Ask children to work together to arrange the lids in ABC order on the masking tape line.

3 When completed, have the groups switch lids so each has an opportunity to work with both upper- and lowercase letters.

Teacher Corner

As children learn this game, add it to a learning center for independent practice. To increase the challenge and develop automaticity, have children time themselves with an egg timer, and record their progress.

12

Consonant Quizzer

Skill: consonants
Players: whole class

Materials

21 small unlined index cards
thick black marker
pen

Getting Ready

🌀 On one side of an index card, print one consonant using a thick black marker.

🌀 On the back of each index card, write a phrase from page 14. Be sure that possible answers to the phrase begin with the letter on the front of the card. For example, for the "b" card you might write the phrase "an animal." Possible answers include *bear, bird,* and *bumble bee*.

🌀 When completed, shuffle the cards.

How to Play

1 Display one card at a time. Children should only see the letter on the front of the card.

2 Read the phrase on the back of the card.

3 Call on volunteers to suggest possible responses to the phrase, using the letter on the card as the first letter of their response.

4 The first child to provide a correct response gets to keep the card.

5 Play continues until all the cards have been used. The child with the most cards wins the game.

Consonant Quizzer
Phrases

a subject in school

something green

a color

a name of a cereal

a place

something at a party

something for breakfast

a kind of fruit

a TV program

something to drink

something to snack on

something in the ocean

something that breaks

something you cook

a kind of fish

something round

something with four wheels

something sharp

an animal

something that smells good

a sport

a boy's name

something that makes noise

something in the kitchen

something hot

something to sit on

something that grows on trees

something good to eat

something with wheels

a story character

something small

something sour

a girl's name

something soft

something to keep you warm

a kind of flower

a winter thing

something made of wood

something you wear

a kind of pet

something you can buy

something square

a kind of dog

a kind of musical instrument

a name of a city or town

something large

something loud

something with feathers

something in the sky

a farm animal

something sweet

something with wings

something to read

a part of the body

a cartoon character

something in the hospital

Soft *c* & *g* Rhyme Bookmarks

Make copies of the bookmarks below for each child. Paste them onto lightweight cardboard. Also write the rhymes on separate sheets of chart paper. Read aloud each rhyme. During a rereading you might choose to use a small musical keyboard with built-in rhythmic patterns. Allow children to repeat the rhyme in several different rap rhythms. Then have them generate a list of words that follow each phonic generalization. Write the words on chart paper for future reference when reading or writing. Invite children to add new words on the back of their bookmarks as well. Also help students to note the exceptions to the generalizations, such as *get* and *give*.

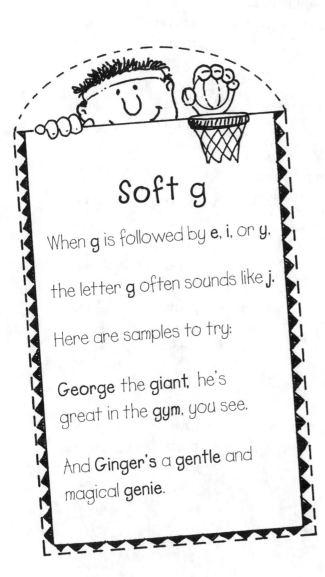

Soft g

When **g** is followed by **e, i,** or **y,**

the letter **g** often sounds like **j.**

Here are samples to try:

George the **giant,** he's great in the **gym,** you see.

And **Ginger's** a **gentle** and magical **genie.**

Soft c

When **c** is followed by **e, i,** or **y,**

the letter **c** often sounds like **s.**

Here are samples to try:

The **city's** in the **cyclone's center,** you see.

And **cereal,** and **cinnamon,** and **celery.**

Consonant Corner

Skill: soft and hard *c* and *g*
Players: whole class

Materials

unlined index cards
thick black marker
construction paper
tape

Getting Ready

🌀 Using a thick black marker and unlined index cards, make a set of soft *c* and hard *c* word cards. Use the word lists here. (Word lists are also provided for soft and hard *g*.)

🌀 Make two construction paper signs, one labeled "soft c" and the other labeled "hard c."

How to Play

1 Designate one corner of the room as the "soft c" corner and another as the "hard c" corner.

2 Distribute one card to each child. Have children read their word cards and quietly go to the appropriate corner. After children have assembled in the corner, ask them to read their words aloud.

3 To continue play, collect the cards, reshuffle, and redistribute.

Soft C	ceiling
celery	cellar
cement	cent
center	cereal
cinnamon	citrus
circle	circus
city	cycle
cyclone	cymbal

Hard C	cat
card	carry
catch	coat
coin	come
cook	corn
cotton	count
cow	cozy
cube	cute

Soft G	gel
gem	general
generous	genie
genius	gentle
geography	George
germ	giant
ginger	giraffe
gym	gypsy

Hard G	game
Gary	gate
gave	get
ghost	girl
give	go
goat	gold
gone	good
gum	guy

Concentration

Skill: soft and hard *g*
Players: 2 to 4

Materials

game cards (see page 18)
scissors

Getting Ready

🌀 Make a copy of the game
cards and cut them out.

🌀 Arrange the cards facedown
on a table.

How to Play

1 In turn, each player turns over two cards and reads
aloud the word or words on each card. If the selected
cards contain a match, such as "soft g" and "gym," the player gets to keep the cards. If the cards do not match, the
player turns the cards over in their original position. The
object of the game is to remember where words are
located so that pairs can be formed in future turns.

2 Each player continues until all the pairs have been
found. The player with the most cards at the end of
the game wins.

Variations

❊ Additional soft and hard
g words can be found on
page 16.

❊ Make Concentration
game cards to reinforce
soft and hard *c*, using the
word lists on page 16.

a gl e fr i th o st u

Concentration
Game Cards

soft g	soft g	soft g	soft g
soft g	giant	gentle	gym
gem	germ	hard g	hard g
hard g	hard g	hard g	gorilla
go	gate	game	goat

Ready-to-Go Phonics Scholastic Professional Books

Blend Match-a-Roo

Skill: consonant clusters
Players: 2 to 4

Materials

game boards (see pages 20–22)
3 pieces of 9- by 12-inch cardboard
glue or paste
black marker
hole punch or sharp pencil
15 pieces of yarn, each 10 inches long
tape

Getting Ready

🐨 Copy the game boards. Paste each game board to a piece of cardboard. On the back of the cardboard, write the name of each picture.

🐨 Punch a hole through the black circles to the right of each consonant cluster. Thread a piece of yarn through each of these holes and secure from the back with a knot. Wrap the loose yarn ends with tape to prevent them from fraying.

🐨 Punch a hole through the black circles to the left of each picture.

How to Play

1 Hand out one Blend Match-a-Roo card to each child.

2 Have children take the attached piece of yarn from the initial consonant cluster and match it to the picture by pushing the yarn end through the hole next to the picture.

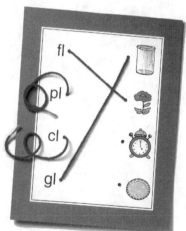

Variations

✳ Additional *r*-blend words include *bread, brick, bride, bridge, brown, brush, crab, crawl, crib, crown, crutches, cry, draw, dress, drip, drum, frown, fruit, fry, grapes, graph, grass, green, grill, groom, pretzel, train, tray, triangle, truck, trunk.*

✳ Additional *l*-blend words include *black, block, blow, blue, clap, clay, cliff, cloud, clowns, flag, flashlight, float, floor, flute, fly, globe, glue, plane, plant, plow, plug, plus.*

✳ Additional *s*-blend words include *skirt, skunk, sled, sleep, slide, smell, smile, smoke, snail, snow, spill, spin, spoon, space, spark, speak, stamp, steam, steps, stir, stop, stump, sweep, swim, swing.*

a gl e fr i th o st u

Phonics Fact: A consonant cluster is a combination of two or more consonants in which the sounds of both letters are blended and heard. Consonant clusters include *r*-blends (*br, gr, pr*), *l*-blends (*bl, cl, fl*), and *s*-blends (*sm, sn, st*).

Oct. 21

Blend Match-a-Roo
r-blends

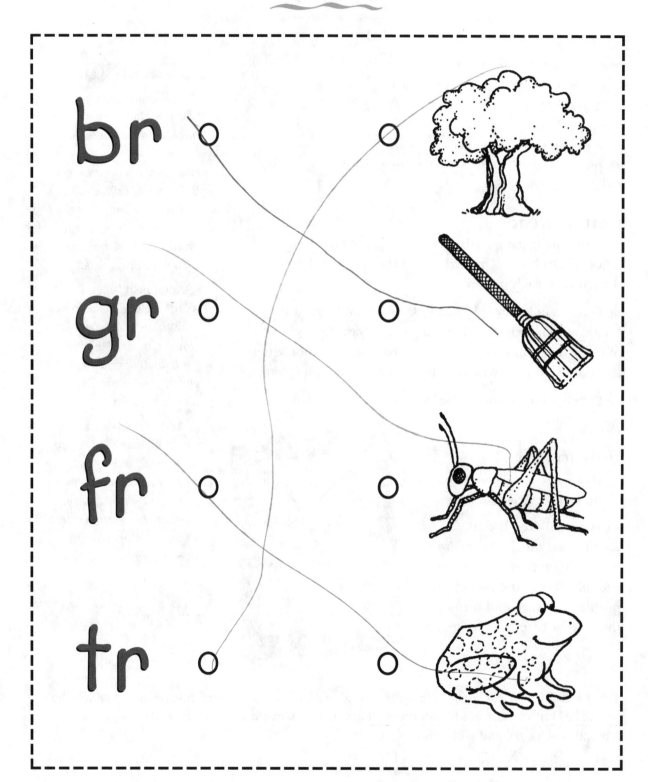

br ○   ○

gr ○   ○

fr ○   ○

tr ○   ○

Blend Match-a-Roo
l-blends

Oct. 21

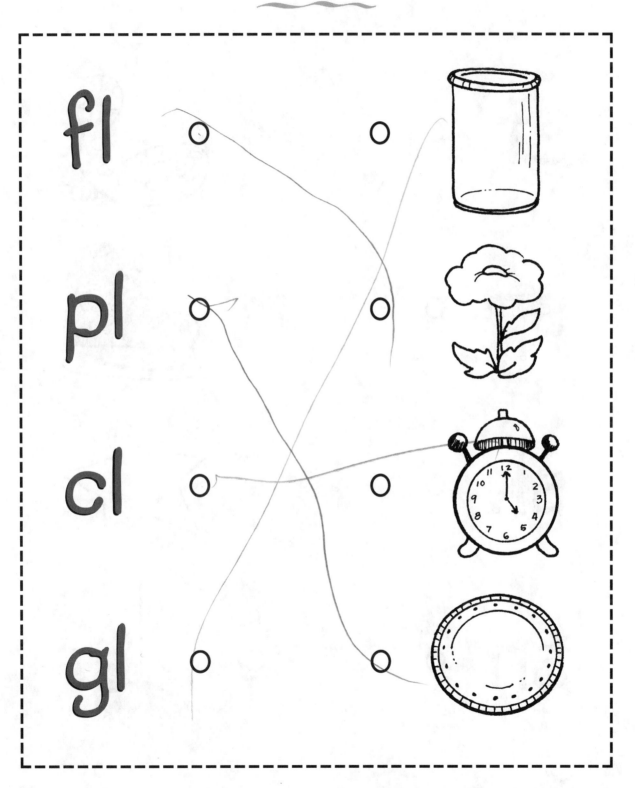

fl   ○   ○

pl   ○   ○

cl   ○   ○

gl   ○   ○

Blend Match-a-Roo

s-blends

Oct. 21

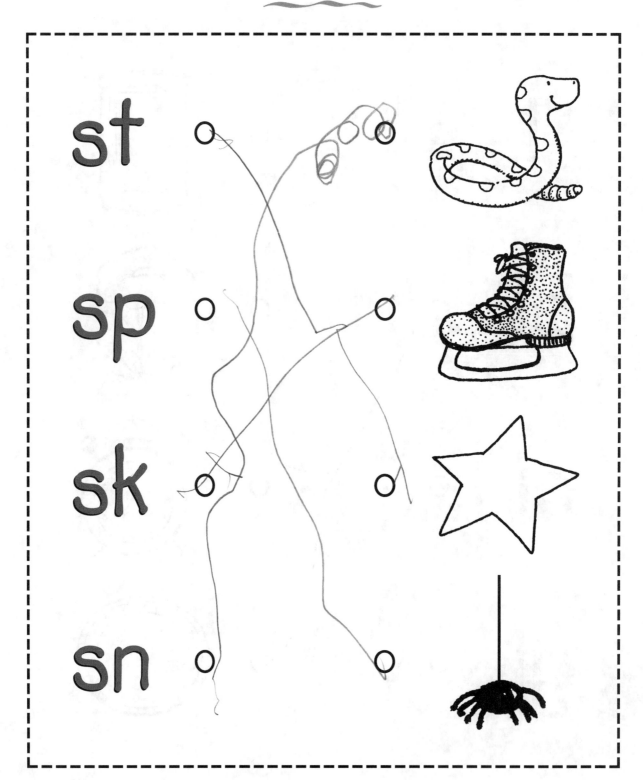

st

sp

sk

sn

Ready-to-Go Phonics Scholastic Professional Books

22

Blend-O

Skill: consonant clusters
Players: any number

Materials

game board (see page 24)
black marker
small slips of paper
paper bag
space markers (or buttons)

Getting Ready

Make enough copies of the game board for each child in your class. Use the words below to fill in the boards. Put the words in a different order on each game board. Also write each word on a small slip of paper and place the slips in a bag.

Game 1: *scar, scout, skate, skunk, small, smart, snail, sneeze, space, spin, star, stop, sweet, swell, scrap, scream, square, squeak, strain, straw, spray, spring, splash, split*

Game 2: *black, blanket, block, blow, clam, class, clear, clock, flag, flash, flip, flower, glass, globe, glove, glue, place, plane, plant, please, sled, sleep, slice, slow*

Game 3: *brain, branch, brick, brown, crash, cry, dragon, drank, free, freeze, frog, fruit, grade, grape, grass, grin, praise, present, price, proud, track, train, tray, truck*

How to Play

1 Blend-O is played just like regular bingo. Give each player a game board and ample space markers. The caller draws one slip of paper from the bag and reads the word aloud.

2 If a player's game board contains that word, he or she places a marker over the space.

3 The first player to get five markers in a row, either vertically, horizontally, or diagonally, yells "Blend-O." The player then reads the words aloud in the row as the caller checks them against the slips of paper drawn from the bag. If these match, the player wins. Players then clear their boards, the slips of paper go back in the bag, and a new game begins.

Variations

Use the following word lists to make game boards for digraphs:

SH *shade, shadow, shake, shape, share, shark, sharp, she, shed, sheep, sheet, shelf, shell, shield, shine, ship, shirt, shock, shoe, shore, should, show, shut, shy*

CH *chain, chair, chalk, chance, change, chapter, chase, cheap, check, cheer, cheese, cherry, chess, chest, chew, chicken, child, chilly, chin, chip, choose, chop, chose, chunk*

WH *what, which, white, whole, whip, whale, who, whisper, wheat, while, whiz, whether, whine, whistle, whirl, whim, whack, whiff, whimper, why, where, when, whose, wheel*

TH *think, thought, thaw, three, though, throw, thick, the, third, there, they, then, thin, than, this, thing, tree, them, that, those, thank, through, these, thread*

a gl e fr i th o st u

Blend-O
Game Board

		Free		

Digraph Rhyme

Write the following rhyme on a sheet of chart paper. (You may also want to reproduce and hand out individual copies to each child.) Read aloud the rhyme. During the first reading, say the letters *c-h, t-h, s-h, w-h, c-k, g-h, n-g,* and *p-h.* During a second reading, say the sound that each digraph stands for—/ch/, /th/, /sh/, /wh/, /k/, /g/, /ng/, and /f/. Then have children generate a list of words that contain each digraph. Write the words on chart paper for future reference when reading and writing. You might choose to use the list to write group stories. To do so, begin with a title that contains the digraph you want to focus on, such as "The King's Ring" or "Sharks!"

Phonics Fact: A consonant digraph is a combination of two consonant letters representing a single consonant sound. The digraphs include *ch, th, sh, wh, ck, gh, ng,* and *ph.*

Digraph Rhyme

Digraphs are two letters
that make a single sound:
ch, th, sh, wh,
together fall upon the ground.
Digraphs are two letters
that make a single sound:
ck, gh, ng, ph
heaped up in a mound.

Digraph Puzzlers

Skill: digraphs
Players: 1 to 2

Materials

game cards (see pages 27–28)
lightweight cardboard or file folders
scissors
glue or paste

Getting Ready

🐾 Copy the game card pages. A blank template is provided to make additional cards.

🐾 Paste the pages to lightweight cardboard or file folders. (Laminate the pages for added durability.) Then cut apart the puzzle pieces by cutting along the inside jagged lines.

How to Play

1 Mix up the puzzle pieces and place them on a table or floor.

2 In turn, each child matches a word with its picture. Children keep each puzzle they correctly complete.

Teacher Corner

Increase the Challenge

Let individuals time themselves, using an egg timer. Have children record the number of puzzles they can complete in a predetermined amount of time.

Make Other Puzzles

Use stickers or old workbook and magazine pictures for the following: *chain, chalk, chart, checkers, cheese, cherry, chess, chest, chicken, children, chimney, chipmunk, chocolate, chop, beach, bench, branch, peach, sandwich, shampoo, shark, shave, sheep, sheet, shell, shirt, shoe, shovel, brush, dish, fish, wash, thermometer, thumb, thermos, thimble, thirteen, three, thistle, bath, moth, teeth, wheel, wheelchair, whistle, king, strong, wing.*

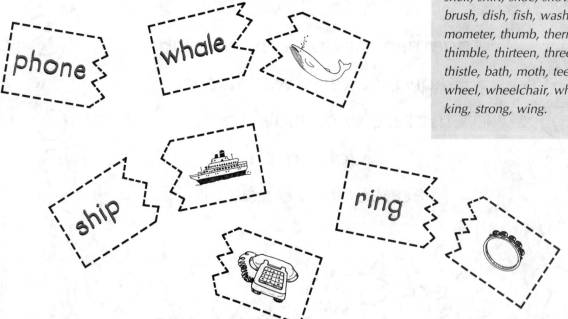

Digraph Puzzlers
Game Cards

ship

chair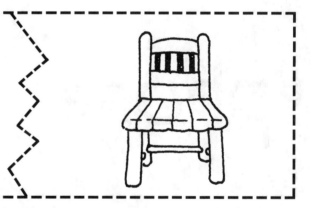

whale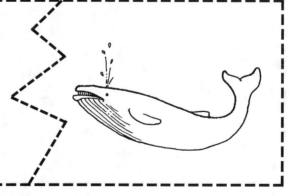

Digraph Puzzlers

Game Cards

ring

phone

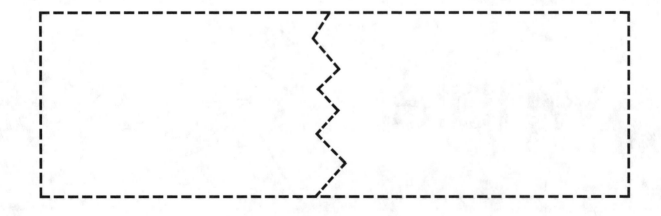

Ready-to-Go Phonics Scholastic Professional Books

Vowel Cheers

To reinforce the short-vowel sounds, teach children the following vowel cheers (pages 29–31). Write the cheers on chart paper and read them aloud. You may also wish to reproduce and distribute copies to each child. The individual letters in the cheers, such as A-a or E-e, should be read as short-vowel sounds. For example, the first line of the "A Cheer" would be read as "/ă/ /ă/—apple." In addition, emphasize any words in the cheers that contain the target short-vowel sound. Encourage children to create motions and actions for each cheer.

Literature Link

To emphasize the importance of vowels in words, read and discuss Shel Silverstein's humorous poem "Importnt?" from *A Light in the Attic* (Harper & Row, 1981).

 Cheer

A-a-apple
Yummy, yummy.
A-a-apple
For the tummy.
A-a-apple
Juicy sweet.
A-a-apple
What a treat!

E Cheer

E-e-eggs
For breakfast, breakfast.
E-e-eggs
From a chicken's nest.
E-e-eggs
All scrambled, scrambled.
E-e-eggs
On toast is the best!

I Cheer

I-i-inchworm
Wiggle, waggle.
I-i-inchworm
Giggle, gaggle.
I-i-inchworm
Loopy, scoopy.
I-i-inchworm
Drippy, droopy!

Ready-to-Go Phonics Scholastic Professional Books

O Cheer

O-o-octopus
Creepy, crawly.
O-o-octopus
Biggy, smally.
O-o-octopus
Squeezy, snugly.
O-o-octopus
Really ugly!

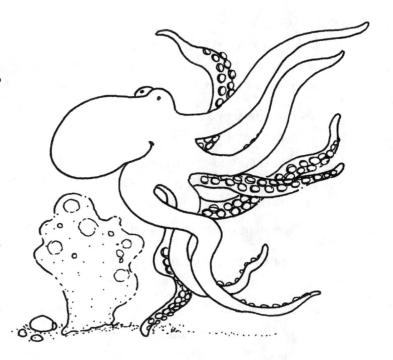

U Cheer

U-u-umbrella
Drip, drip, drop, drop.
U-u-umbrella
Trickle, trickle, plop, plop.
U-u-umbrella
Squishy, squashy.
U-u-umbrella
Wishy, washy!

Short & Long Vowels

Use the word lists on pages 32–36 and the vowel picture cards on page 37 to introduce each vowel and its corresponding long and short sounds. You may also use these pictures and lists for reference during upcoming activities and games.

To use the word lists:

🦜 Make multiple copies of each word list.

🦜 Use the word lists to assess each child's ability to read words with a specific sound. For example, following the Pick 'n' Peek activity on page 39, you might use the short-vowel word lists for assessment.

🦜 You may also wish to send word lists home for additional decoding practice.

To use the picture cards:

🦜 Make multiple copies of the picture cards.

🦜 Cut apart the cards, enlarge them on a photocopier, and decorate as desired.

🦜 Display the cards on a wall in the classroom to create a Word Wall. Have children add words containing each sound under the appropriate picture card.

Short-Vowel Word Lists

Short-*a* Vowel Words

add	cat	had	math	sand
and	dad	ham	nap	stamp
ant	drag	hand	pan	tan
ask	fan	hat	rag	tap
bad	flag	lad	ramp	trash
bag	flap	mad	ran	wag
bat	flat	man	rap	
can	glad	map	rat	
cap	glass	mat	sad	

Short-*e* Vowel Words

bed	den	lent	peck	shell	then
bell	dent	less	pen	sled	vent
belt	dress	let	pest	smell	vest
bend	fed	melt	red	spell	wed
bent	fell	men	rent	spend	well
best	felt	mend	rest	spent	went
cent	get	mess	sell	swell	west
check	help	met	send	tell	wet
chess	hen	neck	sent	ten	when
chest	led	nest	set	tent	wreck
deck	lend	net	shed	test	yell

Short-*i* Vowel Words

bid	fit	kill	sick	still	win
big	flip	kit	sip	thick	zip
bit	grid	lid	sit	tick	
clip	grill	mitt	skin	till	
did	hid	pick	skit	tin	
dig	hip	pig	slick	trip	
fig	hit	pin	slid	twig	
fill	kick	pit	slit	wig	
fin	kid	rip	stick	will	

Ready-to-Go Phonics Scholastic Professional Books

Short-*o* Vowel Words

block	flock	lock	rock	sob
clock	flop	lot	rod	sock
cop	got	mop	rot	spot
cot	hop	nod	shock	stop
crop	hot	not	shop	top
dock	job	pond	shot	
dot	knock	pop	slop	
drop	knot	pot	slot	

Short-*u* Vowel Words

buck	cuff	jump	puff	sun
bud	cup	junk	pump	sunk
bum	cut	just	run	truck
bump	duck	luck	rust	tuck
bun	dump	lump	shut	us
bunk	dust	mud	slump	yum
bus	fun	mutt	stuck	
but	gum	nut	stuff	
chunk	hum	plum	stump	
crust	hut	plump	suds	

Ready-to-Go Phonics Scholastic Professional Books

Long-Vowel Word Lists

Long-*a* Vowel Words

age	came	game	name	save	tame
ape	cape	gate	page	scrape	tape
ate	cave	grade	paid	shade	trace
bake	crate	grape	pain	shake	train
blade	date	hate	pave	shame	wade
blame	drain	lace	place	shape	wage
brace	drape	lake	plate	shave	wake
brain	face	late	quake	snake	wave
brake	fake	made	race	stage	
brave	flake	maid	rain	stain	
cage	flame	main	rake	state	
cake	gain	make	sake	take	

Long-*e* Vowel Words

beam	deed	heap	meal	seal	speak
beat	deep	heat	meat	seat	steal
beef	dream	heel	neat	see	sweep
beep	fee	keen	need	seed	team
beet	feed	keep	peak	seek	treat
clean	feel	knee	peek	seen	weak
cream	gleam	leaf	peep	seep	weed
deal	greed	leap	scream	sleep	week

Long-*i* Vowel Words

bike	glide	lime	ride	time
bite	grime	line	shine	tried
cried	hide	mice	side	vine
crime	hike	mime	slice	white
dice	ice	nice	slide	wide
dime	kite	pine	slime	wife
dried	knife	pipe	spike	wipe
fine	lice	price	strike	write
fried	like	rice	tied	

Long-*o* Vowel Words

boat	float	nose	rope	toad
bone	goat	note	rose	toast
broke	home	phone	smoke	toe
coast	hope	poke	soak	tone
coat	hose	road	soap	tote
cone	joke	roast	sole	vote
doe	load	robe	throat	wrote
dome	mole	rode	throne	

Long-*u* Vowel Words

cube	cute	fuse	mule	mute
cue	fuel	hue	muse	use

Ready-to-Go Phonics Scholastic Professional Books

Vowel Picture Cards

apple

acorn

egg

eagle

inchworm

ice

octopus

overalls

umbrella

unicorn

Ready-to-Go Phonics Scholastic Professional Books

Vowel Spellings

The following chart, provided for your reference, shows vowels and their most common spellings along with key words for each sound. A few of the most frequent spelling patterns, such as -*all* and -*er,* are also included. Use the chart to:

🐿 Emphasize these spellings throughout your instruction.

🐿 Focus on the multiple spellings of specific sounds when children engage in the upcoming games and activities.

🐿 Create a Sound-Spelling Wall in your classroom. Encourage children to add words with each spelling around the chart, grouping them according to sound—for example, short *a,* long *e,* and so on.

/a/	/e/	/i/
h<u>a</u>t	r<u>e</u>d, f<u>e</u>nce, br<u>ea</u>d	p<u>i</u>g, g<u>y</u>m
/o/	/u/	/ā/
t<u>o</u>p	s<u>u</u>n	g<u>a</u>te, h<u>ay</u>, tr<u>ai</u>n
/ē/	/ī/	/ō/
l<u>ea</u>f, tr<u>ee</u>, f<u>ie</u>ld, bab<u>y</u>, monk<u>ey</u>, m<u>e</u>	n<u>i</u>ne, l<u>igh</u>t, fl<u>y</u>, p<u>ie</u>, ch<u>i</u>ld	b<u>o</u>ne, b<u>oa</u>t, pill<u>ow</u>, t<u>oe</u>, g<u>o</u>
/yo͞o/	/o͞o/	/o͝o/
c<u>u</u>be, m<u>u</u>seum, f<u>ew</u>, c<u>ue</u>	br<u>oo</u>m, r<u>u</u>by, tr<u>ue</u>, ch<u>ew</u>, t<u>u</u>ne	b<u>oo</u>k, p<u>u</u>t
/oi/	/ou/	/ô/
b<u>oi</u>l, b<u>oy</u>	h<u>ou</u>se, c<u>ow</u>	b<u>a</u>ll, s<u>aw</u>, s<u>au</u>ce, ch<u>al</u>k, f<u>or</u>k
/ä/	/û/	/â/
c<u>ar</u>, f<u>a</u>ther	g<u>ir</u>l, t<u>ur</u>tle, f<u>er</u>n	ch<u>air</u>, b<u>ear</u>, squ<u>are</u>

Pick 'n' Peek

Skill: short vowels
Players: 2 to 5

Materials
game cards (see pages 39–44)
scissors
hole punch
pencils
tape, glue, or stapler

Getting Ready
🌀 Make an equal number of copies of pages 39–44. Cut out the game cards. Line up the front and back of each card (with the blank sides facing each other), and tape, glue, or staple them together. Laminate, if desired.

🌀 Punch holes where indicated on each card.

🌀 A blank template is provided below to make additional game cards. (For pictures, use stickers or images from old workbooks and magazines. A list of picturable words appears on page 40.)

How to Play
1 Place the cards in the middle of a small group of children, picture-side up. Ask each child to take one card.

2 In turn, have children look at the picture on their card, "pick" the short vowel sound they hear, poke their pencil through the hole next to the letter that stands for that sound, and finally "peek" on the other side of the card to check their response. Children can then swap cards and repeat the activity.

Game Card Front

Pick 'n' Peek
Word List

bag	bed	bib	block	brush
basket	bell	brick	box	bug
bat	belt	chin	chop	bun
cab	desk	dig	clock	bus
can	dress	dish	dock	crust
cat	egg	fin	doll	cup
fan	hen	fish	dot	cut
glass	jet	gift	fox	drum
grass	leg	hill	hop	duck
ham	neck	kick	knot	gum
lamp	nest	lid	lock	hut
man	pen	lip	mom	nut
map	red	milk	ox	plus
plant	shell	mitt	pond	rug
rat	sled	pig	pop	run
sad	ten	pin	rock	skunk
sand	tent	ship	sock	sun
stamp	vest	stick	stop	truck
van	web	swim	top	up

Card Back

○ a

○ e

○ i

○ o

○ u

Ready-to-Go Phonics Scholastic Professional Books

Pick 'n' Peek
Game Cards

Ready-to-Go Phonics Scholastic Professional Books

Pick 'n' Peek
Game Cards

○ a
○ e
○ i
○ o
○ u yes

sun

○ a yes
○ e
○ i
○ o
○ u

cat

○ a
○ e
○ i
○ o yes
○ u

box

Ready-to-Go Phonics Scholastic Professional Books

Pick 'n' Peek

Game Cards

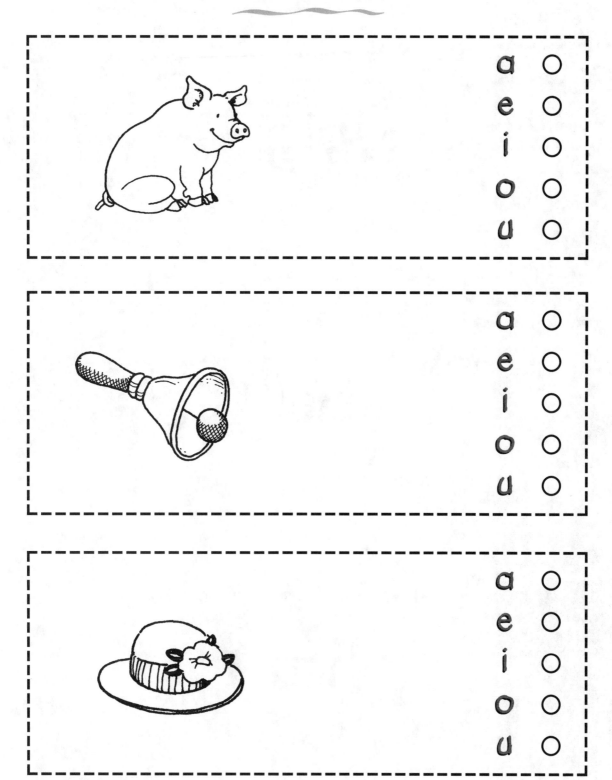

Pick 'n' Peek
Game Cards

○ a
○ e
○ i yes
○ o
○ u

pig

○ a
○ e yes
○ i
○ o
○ u

bell

○ a yes
○ e
○ i
○ o
○ u

hat

Ready-to-Go Phonics Scholastic Professional Books

Old MacDonald's Vowel Farm

Hand out a copy of the song "Old MacDonald's Vowel Farm" to each child. Also write the song on chart paper. Explain to children that this is a different version of the popular song "Old MacDonald Had a Farm." Track the print as you sing. Sing the song several times. During each singing, replace the animal name and corresponding vowel sound. You might choose to use the following animals: hen (/e/), pig (/i/), fox (/o/), and duck (/u/).

Old MacDonald's Vowel Farm

Old MacDonald had a farm–a, e, i, o, u.

And on that farm he had a cat–a, e, i, o, u.

With an a–a here,

And an a–a there.

Here an a,

There an a,

Everywhere an a–a.

Old MacDonald had a farm–a, e, i, o, u!

Vowel Clip It

Skill: short vowels
Players: 1 to 2

Materials

game boards (see pages 47–49)
scissors
3 large manila envelopes
glue or paste
18 spring-type clothespins
black marker
unlined index cards (for answer cards)

Getting Ready

🕊 Make copies of each game board and cut them out. Paste one game board to the front of a manila envelope.

🕊 Write one short vowel on each clothespin to correspond with the missing letter of each word on the game board. (Make sure the vowels read correctly when the clothespins are clipped to the game board.)

🕊 Place an answer card in each envelope to make the game self-checking.

How to Play

1 Have children "clip" the correct vowel clothespin to the blank space in each word on the envelope.

2 Ask children to read the words aloud to you or a student partner.

3 When the game is completed, have children store the clothespins inside the envelope.

Variations

❊ To make additional game boards, cut out magazine pictures that show busy scenes. Using each picture, locate any short-vowel words or concepts that would fit the scene. For example, a barnyard scene might be described using short-vowel words such as *chicken, pig,* and *nest*. Write the words at the top or bottom edge of the envelope, leaving a blank for the short vowel.

❊ Make game boards containing long-vowel, variant vowel (oo), diphthong (ou, ow, oi, oy), and *r*-controlled-vowel (ar, er, ir, or, ur) pictures and concepts.

gl e fr i th o st u

Vowel Clip It
Game Board

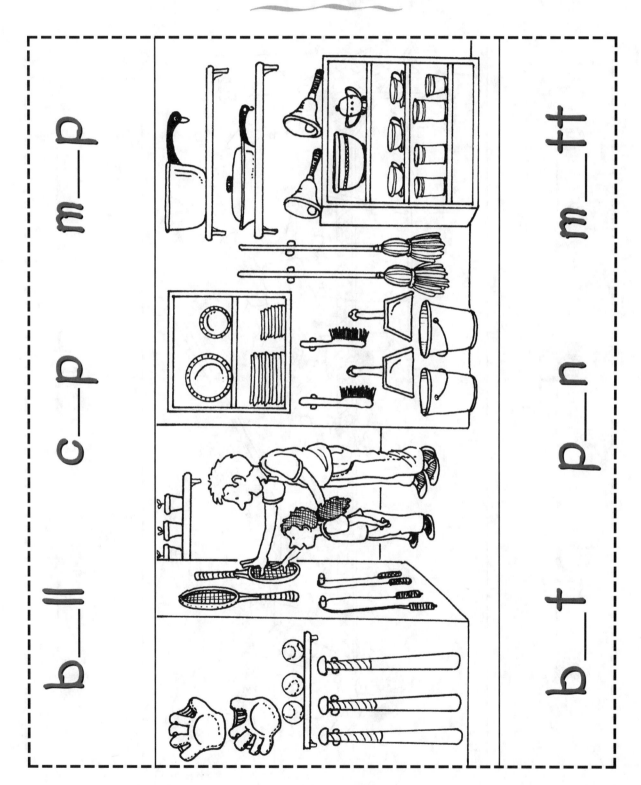

m — p

c — p

b — ll

m — tt

p — n

b — t

Vowel Clip It
Game Board

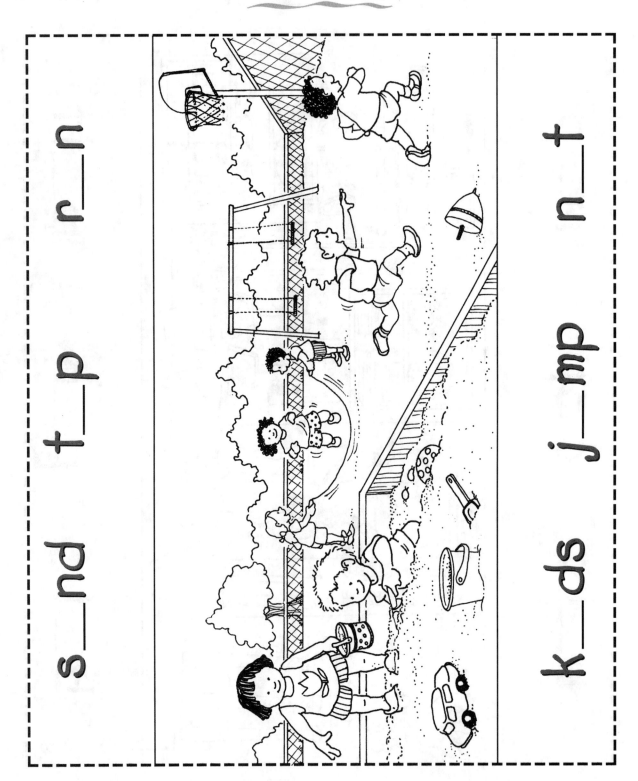

r_n   t_p   s_nd

n_t   j_mp   k_ds

Vowel Clip It
Game Board

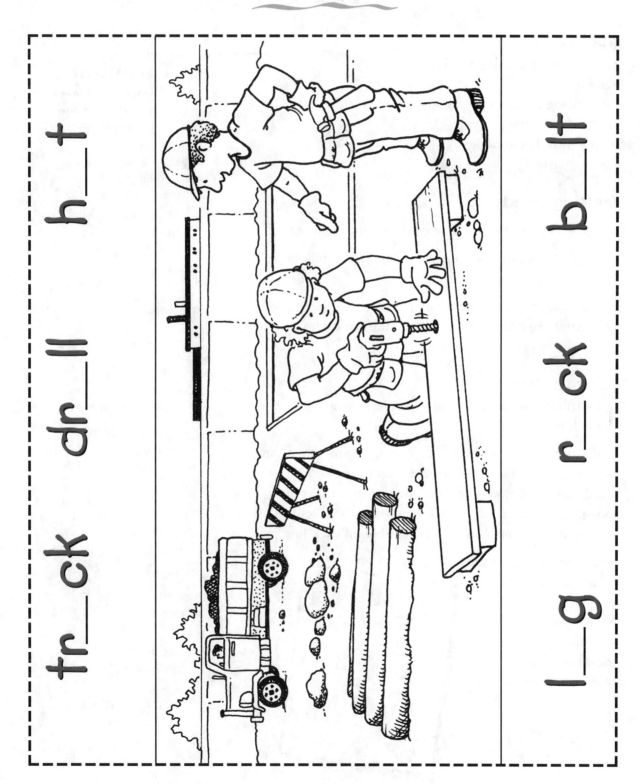

tr _ ck   dr _ ll   h _ t

l _ g   r _ ck   b _ lt

Vowel-in-the-Middle

Skill: short vowels
Players: 1 to 4

Materials

game cards (see pages 51-52)
scissors
10 milk jug lids or small tagboard circles
thick black marker
2 large manila envelopes
glue or paste

Getting Ready

❧ Make copies of each game card and cut them out.

❧ Write the short vowels *a, e, i, o,* and *u* on milk jug lids—one letter per lid.

❧ For easy storage, paste each game card on the outside of a manila envelope. Place milk jug lids for each vowel inside the envelope.

How to Play

1 Distribute a game card and vowel lids to each group of children.

2 In turn, each child places a vowel in the middle of one line on the game card to make a familiar word. The child must read aloud the word formed to earn a point. One point is earned for each correct word. Challenge children to make as many words as possible on each line.

3 Play continues in this fashion until all lines of the game cards have been used. The player with the most points at the end of the game wins.

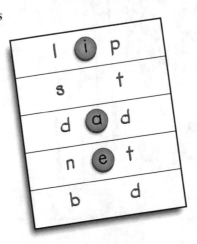

Variations

✿ Make multiple copies of each game card. Have students write a vowel to complete each word.

✿ Make additional game cards using the following incomplete words:

Short Vowels
Game 1
b_g, b_t, t_n, r_g, t_p

Game 2
p_n, r_t, m_n, h_m, d_g

Game 3
s_n, p_g, c_t, m_p, b_d

Game 4
b_s, s_t, c_p, l_t, p_p

Game 5
m_t, b_m, n_t, b_s, p_t

Other Vowels
Write the following vowel digraphs on milk jug lids for the following games:
ai, ay, ea, ee, oa, ow, oo, ou, oi.

Game 1
tr_n, b_k, b_n, l_t, r_d

Game 2
s_l, r_t, r_m, s_p, t_n

Game 3
s_d, p_n, pl_y, m_n, l_d

Game 4
l_k, z_m, t_d, r_n, pr_d

Game 5
m_t, l_f, c_t, br_t, n_t

Vowel-in-the-Middle
Game Card

l	p
s	t
d	d
n	t
b	d

Vowel-in-the-Middle
Game Card

c	p
f	n
h	m
m	t
z	p

Ready-to-Go Phonics Scholastic Professional Books

Treasure Sock

Distribute one copy of the poem "Treasure Sock" to each child. Read aloud the poem. Then ask students to underline each word containing a short-vowel sound. Record children's responses on chart paper, creating a chart for each short-vowel sound—/a/, /e/, /i/, /o/, /u/. Continue the activity with other poems.

Treasure Sock

One day while I was walking
I found a pretty rock.
I picked it up and checked it out
Then put it in my sock.

I came upon a penny,
And then a piece of string,
A rusty cap, a tiny screw,
A bent-up shiny thing.

I sat down in a grassy patch,
Took off one buckled shoe,
Rolled down my sock and took it off,
Then knew what I could do.

I picked up all my findings
And placed them with my rock.
I proudly took it home to mom
And showed off my treasure sock!

Say It and Slot It

Skill: long vowels
Players: 1 to 4

Materials

shoe box with lid
scissors
marker
cardboard
picture cards (see page 55)

Getting Ready

🐦 Make five slots in the lid of a shoebox—one for each long-vowel sound. Label each slot "long *a*," "long *e*," "long *i*," "long *o*," and "long *u*," as shown.

🐦 Make cardboard dividers to fit inside the box. Measure and cut four strips of cardboard about an inch longer than the width of the box. The strips should also be a bit narrower than the height of the box. Fold back the ends of each strip, and tape them inside the box as shown. Label each section with the appropriate long-vowel sound. The dividers will keep the cards separated when children drop them through the slots in the lid.

🐦 Make copies of the picture cards. Write the picture names on the back of the cards as well as the appropriate long-vowel sound.

How to Play

1 Place the picture cards faceup on a table.

2 In turn, each player selects one card and places it in the correct slot on the shoe box. For example, the picture of the train would be placed in the "long *a*" slot. Children can check their responses by reading the picture name on the back of the card.

3 Play continues until all the cards have been slotted.

Variation

✿ Paste stickers or old workbook illustrations to index cards to make additional picture cards for the following:

beach, bean, blow, bone, bow, cage, chain, cheese, clay, coat, cone, cry, dice, dive, face, five, game, globe, grapes, green, hay, hive, hose, ice, key, knee, knife, mice, nose, peach, plane, plate, queen, rain, rake, road, rope, rose, sheep, skate, slide, smile, snail, soap, teeth, tie, tree, vase, vine, wave, whale.

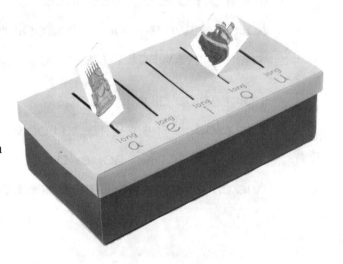

Say It and Slot It
Picture Cards

Silent-*e* Game

Skill: long vowels
Players: 2 to 4

Materials
game board (see pages 58–59)
tape
crayons or markers
scissors
number cube pattern (see page 57)
place marker for each player (or buttons)

Getting Ready

🐦 Make a copy of the two game board pages. Tape together the two halves of the game board along the dotted lines. Color and decorate as desired.

🐦 Copy and cut out the number cube pattern along the dotted lines. Construct the cube by folding along the solid lines and using tape to attach the cube tabs to the cube squares.

How to Play

1 Each player chooses a place marker and puts it on START.

2 The first player throws the number cube and moves his or her marker along the game board path the number of spaces shown on the cube.

3 The player must then read aloud the word on the square he or she has landed on and the word that is formed when a "silent *e*" is added. If the player is unable to state both words, he or she skips a turn.

4 Each player continues in turn. The first player to reach FINISH wins.

Silent-*e* Game
Number Cube

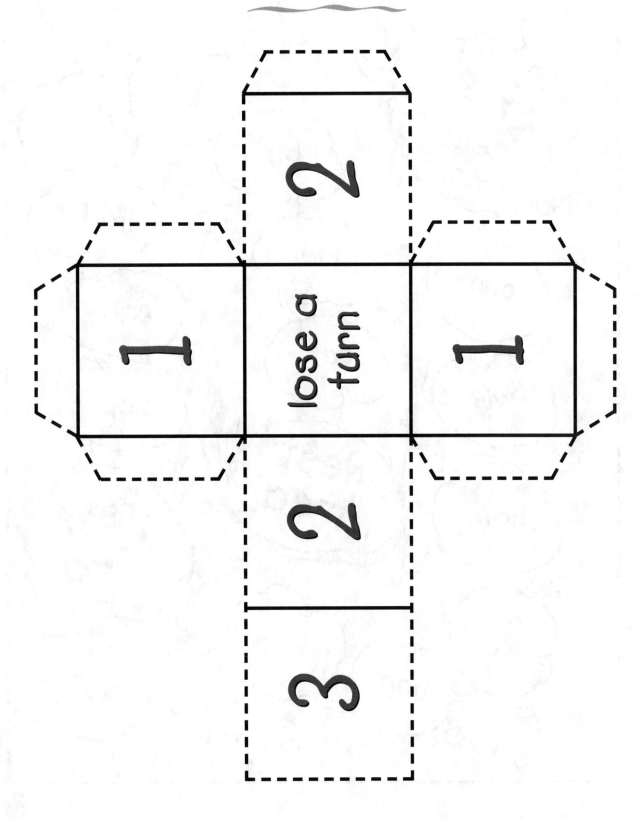

Silent-*e* Game

Silent-*e* Game

Word Score

Skill: vowels
Players: any number

Materials

game board (see page 61)
scissors
6 blue unlined 3" x 5" index cards
5 yellow unlined 3" x 5" index cards
black marker

Getting Ready

🌀 Make multiple copies of the game board.

🌀 Cut each of the six blue index cards into fourths to create 24 cards. Write one of the following consonants on each card: *g, p, n, v, h, f, y, l, w, b, j, k, r, m, s, d, c.* Make two cards for *b, f, r, m, s, d,* and *c.*

🌀 Cut each of the five yellow index cards into fourths to create 20 cards. Write one of the following long-vowel phonograms on each card: *ace, ain, ake, ame, ay, eak, ean, eat, eed, eep, ide, ight, ike, ine, y, oat, oke, old, one, ow.*

🌀 Shuffle the 24 blue consonant cards and evenly place them on the left-hand column spaces (six per space). Shuffle the 20 yellow phonogram cards and evenly place them on the right-hand column spaces (five per space).

Variations

✿ Replace the consonant cards with the following consonant clusters and digraphs: *sh, sl, st, sm, sn, sp, sc, sw, str, spr, gl, gr, bl, dr, wh, pr, pl, fl, fr, ch, cr, cl, th, tr.*

✿ Replace the long-vowel phonograms with the following short-vowel phonograms: *ab, ack, am, an, ap, at, ell, en, est, et, it, ill, ip, od, op, ot, um, un, up, ut.*

a gl e fr i th o st u

How to Play

1 The first player chooses one blue and one yellow card. If the player can make a word using the cards, he or she reads the word aloud. The player then keeps the cards and adds the point value for each card to determine his or her total points earned. The numbers to the left or right of each box indicate the point values. For example, if the player chooses a blue card worth 4 points and a yellow card worth 6 points, the player earns 10 points.

2 Each player continues in turn. The game ends when no more words can be made. The player with the most points wins.

Phonics Fact: A phonogram (or word family) is a letter (or series of letters) that stands for a sound, syllable, or series of sounds without reference to meaning. For example, the phonogram -ee contains two letters and stands for the long-e sound. It can be found in words such as *see, tree,* and *agree.*

Word Score
Game Board

0

6

4

3

5

7

2

1

Diphthong Song

Write "Diphthong Song" on chart paper. You may also wish to make a photocopy for each child. Read it aloud or sing it to the tune of "I'm a Little Teapot." Afterward, have children generate a list of words containing each diphthong —*oi, oy, ou, ow.* Possible words include the following:

OI *noise, voice, oil, broil, spoil, join, choice, joint, coin, soil, foil, coil*

OY *toy, boy, joy, destroy, employ, loyal, annoy, royal, oyster*

OU *scout, cloud, scour, house, ouch, pouch, shout, doubt, count, mouth, hound, foul, lounge, found*

OW *powder, brown, towel, power, chowder, town, drown, clown, crown, shower, vowel*

Phonics Fact: A diphthong is a sound in which the position of the mouth changes as the sound is produced. The sounds *oi* and *ou* are commonly classified as diphthongs.

Literature Links

Use the following to review and highlight words with diphthongs:

Poems "Ounce and Bounce" and "Boing! Boing! Squeak" from *The New Kid on the Block* by Jack Prelutsky (Greenwillow, 1984)

Books *Counting Cows* by Woody Jackson (Harcourt Brace, 1995) and *The Cat Who Wouldn't Come Down* by Paul Brett Johnson (Orchard Books, 1993)

Songs "She'll Be Comin' 'Round the Mountain" and "The Wheels on the Bus"

Diphthong Song

I'm a little diphthong.

Holy cow!

Oi and oy,

ou and ow.

Listen as your voice

glides along each vowel.

I'm a little diphthong.

Holy cow!

Ready-to-Go Phonics Scholastic Professional Books

Dial-a-Diphthong

Skill: diphthongs
Players: 2 to 4

Materials

spinner (see page 64)
scissors
glue or paste
tagboard or file folder
brass fastener
game board (see page 65)
crayons or water–based markers

Getting Ready

Copy and cut out the spinner and dial. Paste the spinner onto a piece of tagboard or the inside of a file folder.

Using a brass fastener, attach the dial to the spinner. (You might also want to make the dial from tagboard.)

Make multiple copies of the game board. You might choose to laminate the game boards so they can be reused. (A blank template is provided to make additional game boards.)

How to Play

1 In turn, each player spins the spinner and states aloud the diphthong, such as *oy*. The player then uses the diphthong to complete a word on his or her game board. If the player spins "your choice," the player can complete any word on the game board using any diph-thong.

2 Each player continues in turn until a player has completed all the words on the game board. That player calls out "Holy cow!" and is the winner.

Variation

The following incomplete words can be used to make additional game boards:

cl__n, p__der, h__se, n__, d__n, h__r, __ster, sh__er, sp__l, br__n, j__n, sh__t, f__l, c__nt, ch__ce, br__n, p__ch, fr__n, b__l, v__ce, sc__t, empl__, cl__d, t__, p__nd, sc__r, d__bt, n__se, t__n, __ch, l__al, m__ntain, J__, h__nd, v__el, c__n, __l, c__, cr__n, s__l, ch__der, dr__n, r__.

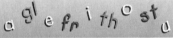

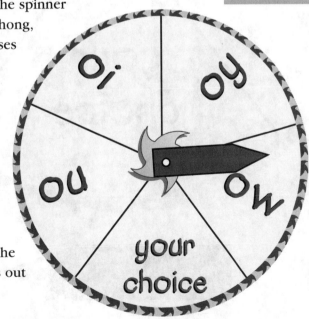

gl fr a th st e tr pl i ch sk o gr ol u wh sp

Dial-a-Diphthong
Spinner

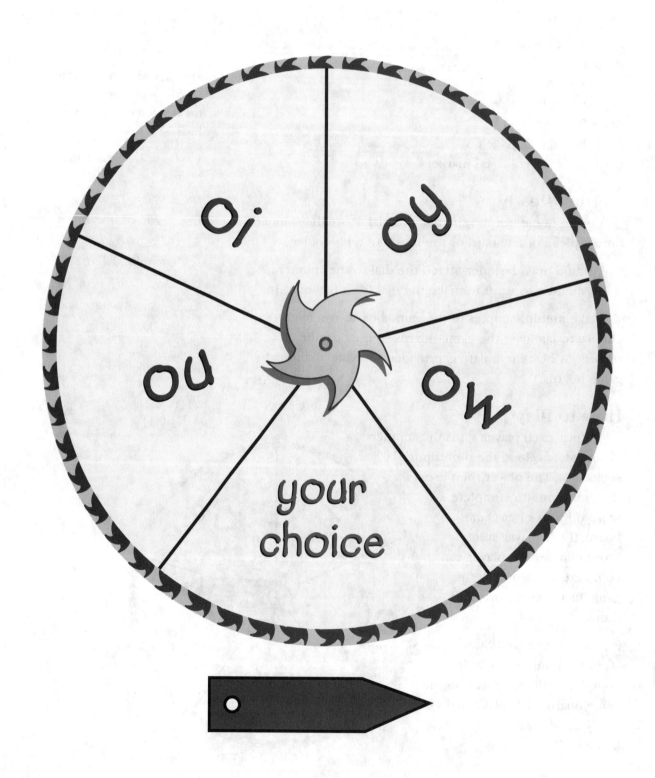

Within the spinner: oi, oy, ou, ow, your choice

gl fr a th st e tr pl i ch sk o gr ol u wh sp

64

Ready-to-Go Phonics Scholastic Professional Books

Dial-a-Diphthong
Game Board

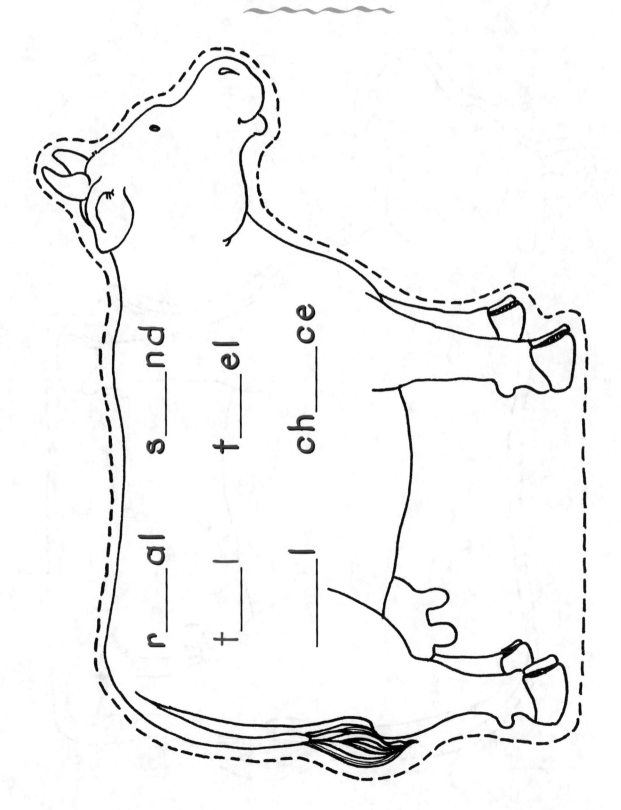

r __ al   s __ nd

t __ l   t __ el

ch __ ce   l __ l

Dial-a-Diphthong
Game Board

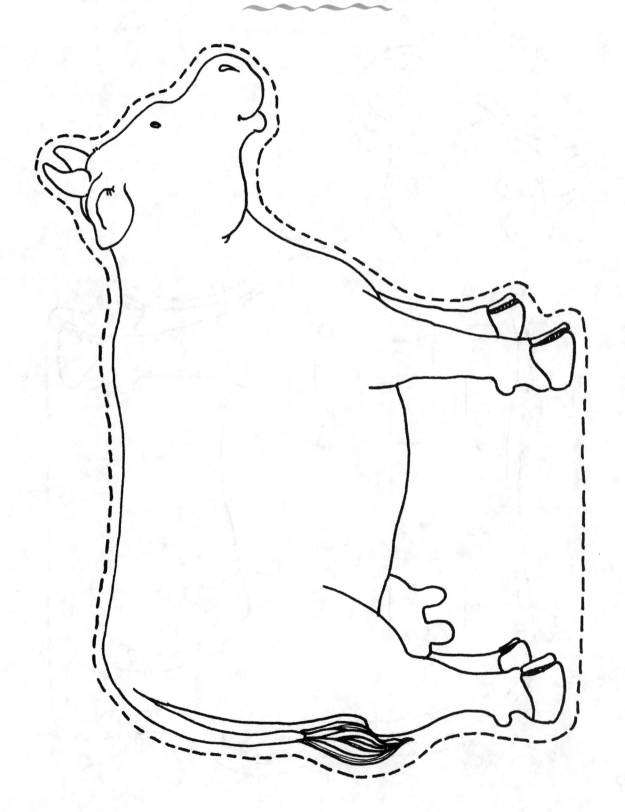

66

Mr. Drew

R eproduce and hand out copies of the poem "Mr. Drew." Write the poem on chart paper and read it aloud. On repeated readings, ask students to clap every time they hear a word with the variant vowel sound / $\overline{oo}$ / as in *chew*. Then have students circle all the words with / $\overline{oo}$ /. Discuss the many spellings for this sound. Challenge students to use these words to create their own / $\overline{oo}$ / poems.

Mr. Drew

I have a dog named Mr. Drew.

I named him after my Uncle Lou.

The problem is, he likes to chew.

(I mean my dog, not Uncle Lou.)

The other day he shredded my shoe.

Wouldn't you know, they were brand-new!

It couldn't be fixed with super-stick glue.

To make matters worse, he wasn't through.

He chewed my tie and a chair leg, too.

There's plenty more, I've just named a few.

When your dog's like that, what can you do?

Ship him off to a faraway zoo?

Send him to your mean nephew?

I wonder if he'd like my Uncle Lou?

My last resort is Timbuktu!

Is man's best friend really a dog?

It depends on your point of view.

Ready-to-Go Phonics Scholastic Professional Books

The Yarn Game

Skill: *r*-controlled vowels
Players: 2 to 4

Materials
game board (see pages 70–71)
tape
colored markers
scissors
number cube (see page 57)
game cards (see page 69)
place marker for each player (or buttons)

Getting Ready
🐾 Make a copy of the game board pages. Tape together the two halves of the game board along the dotted line. Color and decorate as desired.

🐾 Copy and cut out the number cube along the dotted lines. Construct the cube by folding along the solid lines and using tape to attach the cube tabs to the cube squares.

🐾 Copy and cut out the game cards. Place them facedown on the "Pick a W-card" square on the game board.

How to Play
1 Each player chooses a place marker and puts it on START.

2 The first player throws the number cube, moves his or her marker along the game board path the number of spaces shown on the cube, and reads aloud the word. If the player is unable to state the word, he or she skips a turn. If the player lands on the "Pick a W-card" square, he or she must select a "W-card" and read aloud the word. If the student is unable to read the word, he or she must follow the directions on the card.

3 Each player continues in turn. The first player to reach FINISH wins.

Variation
Replace the *ar* words on the game board with the following *r*-controlled-vowel words:

ER her, verse, camera, allergy, over, after, operate, sister, other, better, wonderful, liberty, battery, certain, clerk, ever, letter, mother, herd, person, under, winter

IR girl, bird, first, shirt, dirt, thirsty, firm, sir, fir, quirk, flirt, circle, circus, birth, chirp, dirty, thirteen, skirt, squirm, stir, third, twirl

UR slurp, nurse, church, purse, purple, Thursday, curb, hurt, surface, purpose, blur, burn, churn, curl, curve, fur, purr, spur, surf, turkey, turn, turtle

OR cork, fork, more, pork, port, horn, corn, corner, tore, torn, dorm, form, sore, chore, wore, orphan, sports, organ, born, for, horse, short

a gl e fr i th o st u

The Yarn Game
Game Cards

warm lose a turn	**warn** go back 2 spaces	**warmth** lose a turn
warp go back 1 space	**warning** lose a turn	**warm-up** move ahead 2 spaces
ward move ahead 1 space	**warrior** go back 1 space	**warming** lose a turn
wart lose a turn	**war** go back 3 spaces	**warden** move ahead 2 spaces

The Yarn Game

Ready-to-Go Phonics Scholastic Professional Books

join game board here

The Yarn Game

The ABC's of Compound Words

Challenge small groups of children to brainstorm one compound word for each letter of the alphabet. Suggest that they write each word in a sentence on a separate sheet of construction paper and illustrate it. They can then bind the pages to make an ABC's of Compound Words book. As an alternative, you might assign each student one page to complete. Below are possible word choices.

A	afternoon	**J**	jackknife	**S**	sandpaper
B	baseball	**K**	keyboard	**T**	tattletale
C	catfish	**L**	landslide	**U**	upstairs
D	doghouse	**M**	mailbox	**V**	volleyball
E	eardrum	**N**	newspaper	**W**	wallpaper
F	football	**O**	oatmeal	**X**	X-ray
G	girlfriend	**P**	pancake	**Y**	yardstick
H	haircut	**Q**	quicksand	**Z**	zigzag
I	iceberg	**R**	raincoat		

Compound Art

Have children generate a list of compound words. List the words on chart paper and categorize them. Categories might include sports (*football, baseball, basketball*), household items (*cupboard, bathroom, highchair*), food (*hotdog, cupcake, oatmeal*), winter (*snowplow, snowman, snowsuit*), outdoor things (*treehouse, driveway, lawnmower*), or school (*stairway, lunchroom, playground*). When completed, encourage children to select ten words to use in a short story or poem. Instead of writing the compound word in the story, suggest that they add an illustration of each word part so that the reader can guess it. For example:

I saw a  in the sky.

As an alternative, have children create compound-word pages for their classmates. Show children the compound art for the word *rainbow* on page 73 as an example. When completed, make copies of children's pages and place them in a learning center for class use.

Compound Art
Activity Page

 +  = rainbow

 +  =

 + 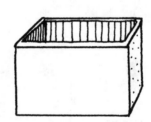 = _____

 +  = _____

Compound Comedy

Make multiple copies of the Compound Comedy strips on pages 74-75. Divide the class into groups of 3 to 4 children and distribute one strip to each group. Challenge groups to write a humorous short story using as many words as possible from their strip. When completed, have groups share their stories. Invite children to compile the stories and bind them to form a Compound Comedy class book.

Compound Comedy #1
grandpa
earthquake
suitcase
haircut
overcoat
toothbrush
drugstore
eyeball
rowboat
cookbook

Compound Comedy #2
cupcake
girlfriend
headache
sweatshirt
toenail
lipstick
lifeboat
jellyfish
barefoot
birthday

Ready-to-Go Phonics Scholastic Professional Books

Compound Comedy #3

backyard
fruitcake
policeman
midnight
highway
haystack
screwdriver
windshield
flashlight
toothpick

Compound Comedy #4

outdoors
upstairs
notebook
homework
fireplace
wristwatch
blackout
newspaper
thunderstorm
weekend

Compound Comedy #5

afternoon
sailboat
goldfish
airplane
rainbow
dragonfly
daytime
overalls
overboard
waterfall

Compound Comedy #6

playpen
highchair
doorway
silverware
ponytail
dishpan
applesauce
outfit
bathtub
shoelace

Contraction Pop-Ups

Skill: contractions
Players: whole class

Materials
20 tongue depressors or craft sticks
20 small unlined index cards
black marker
small can

Getting Ready
🌀 Write each of the following word pairs on a tongue depressor: *I am, could not, are not, what is, did not, have not, you are, was not, will not, should not, they are, you have, he is, you will, who will, it is, they will, would not, I have, let us.* Place the tongue depressors in a small can.

🌀 Write each of the sentences listed to the right on index cards, one sentence per card.

How to Play

1 Distribute one index card to each child.

2 In turn, have a volunteer select one tongue depressor from the can and read aloud the two words written on it. The child whose index card sentence contains a contraction that can be formed from the two words "pops up" and reads aloud the sentence. Continue until all the tongue depressors have been selected.

you are

who will

let us

should not

I'm going to the park today.

David couldn't find his math book.

Those green shoes aren't mine.

What's the matter with you?

You didn't eat all of your lunch.

They haven't come home yet.

You're my best friend.

Mary wasn't in the car.

My dog won't bite.

You shouldn't play in the street.

They're waiting in the gray van.

You've more pencils than Maria.

He's the fastest runner.

You'll be late for school.

Who'll help me?

It's time for our dinner.

They'll paint the house yellow.

I wouldn't want to go.

I've a surprise in that box.

Let's go to a movie today.

Contraction Toss

Skill: contractions
Players: any number

Materials

white or light-colored plastic tablecloth
thick black marker
masking tape
large coffee can lid

Getting Ready

🌀 Using a thick black marker, randomly write the following contractions on the plastic tablecloth: *aren't, can't, couldn't, doesn't, don't, hadn't, hasn't, he'd, he'll, he's, here's, I'd, I'll, I'm, I've, isn't, let's, she'd, she'll, she's, shouldn't, that's, there's, they'll, they've, wasn't, we'd, we'll, we're, we've, weren't, what's, who's, won't, wouldn't, you'd, you'll, you're, you've.*

🌀 Secure the tablecloth to the floor with masking tape.

How to Play

1 In turn, each player tosses the lid onto the tablecloth. The player then reads any word that the lid touches or covers. One point is earned for each word correctly read.

2 Play continues in this fashion. The player with the most points at the end of the game wins.

Syllable Search

Syllabication Computation #1

Review with children how to count the number of syllables in a word. Read aloud the following words, and help children as they count the number of syllables in each:

1 syllable: lunch, home, school, desk

2 syllables: funny, tower, rabbit, diet

3 syllables: crocodile, hurricane, carpenter, orchestra

4 syllables: alligator, indigestion, transportation, complicated

5 syllables: flexibility, auditorium, contemporary, superintendent

Divide the class into groups of 3 or 4 children. Provide each group with a sheet of paper. Challenge each group to write a list of words whose total number of syllables adds up to 10. When completed, have groups read their words for the class to check. Compare the number of words used by each group. Which group used the fewest words? How many 3-, 4-, or 5-syllable words did each group use? Continue play by increasing the number of syllables.

team 2
Mia
Todd
Ayesha
Lily

airplane
teacher
pencil
recess
desk
run

gl fr a th st e tr pl i ch sk o gr cl u wh sp

Syllabication Computation #2

Write the following on the chalkboard. Have groups of 3 or 4 children work together to fill in the blanks for one of the challenges. You might suggest that they search classroom books for words.

🦃 Find 4 one-syllable words _____ , _____ , _____ , _____ .

🦃 Find 2 two-syllable wordss _____ , _____ .

🦃 Find 3 three-syllable words _____ , _____ , _____ .

🦃 Find 4 four-syllable words _____ , _____ , _____ , _____ .

🦃 Find 3 five-syllable words _____ , _____ , _____ .

🦃 Find 1 six-syllable word _____ .

Total: 54 syllables

Syllabication Computation #3

Distribute a copy of a short poem, such as "Pollution," below. Have children count the total number of syllables in the poem. (28) You might have children work in small groups. Provide time for each group to report their results. Extend the activity by inviting children to count the number of syllables in other short poems.

Pollution

When my dad comes home from work,

He relaxes in his chair.

Then he slips his big shoes off

And his socks pollute the air!

Classroom Resources

Fun Phonics Manipulatives: Quick and Easy Flip-Books, Pull-Throughs and Interactive Mini-Books to Make and Share by Michelle Hancock, Sheryl Pate, and Jennie VanHaelst (Scholastic, 1998).

Phonics from A to Z: A Practical Guide by Wiley Blevins (Scholastic, 1998).

Phonics for the Teacher of Reading by Marion Hull (Merrill, 1994).

Phonics That Work! by Janiel Wagstaff (Scholastic, 1994).

Phonics They Use: Words for Reading and Writing by Patricia Cunningham (HarperCollins, 1995).

Quick-and-Easy Learning Centers: Phonics by Mary Beth Spann (Scholastic, 1996).

Quick-and-Easy Learning Games: Phonics by Wiley Blevins (Scholastic, 1996).

Strategies for Word Identification: Phonics From a New Perspective by Barbara Fox (Prentice-Hall, 1996).

Teaching and Assessing Phonics: Why, What, When, How by Jeanne Chall and Helen Popp (Educators Publishing Service, 1996).